# First World War
## and Army of Occupation
# War Diary
## France, Belgium and Germany

16 DIVISION
47 Infantry Brigade
Welsh Regiment
18th Battalion
27 July 1918 - 31 May 1919

WO95/1971/3

The Naval & Military Press Ltd
www.nmarchive.com
**Published in association with The National Archives**

Published by

## The Naval & Military Press Ltd

Unit 10 Ridgewood Industrial Park,

Uckfield, East Sussex,

TN22 5QE England

Tel: +44 (0) 1825 749494

www.naval-military-press.com

www.nmarchive.com

*This diary has been reprinted in facsimile from the original. Any imperfections are inevitably reproduced and the quality may fall short of modern type and cartographic standards.*

**© Crown Copyright**
**Images reproduced by permission of The National Archives, London, England, 2015.**

# Contents

| Document type | Place/Title | Date From | Date To |
|---|---|---|---|
| Heading | WO95/1971/3 | | |
| Heading | 16th Division 47th Infy Bde 18th Bn Welsh Regt Jly 1918-May 1919 | | |
| War Diary | Aldershot | 27/07/1918 | 29/07/1918 |
| War Diary | Boulogne | 30/07/1918 | 31/07/1918 |
| War Diary | Bezinghem | 01/08/1918 | 30/08/1918 |
| War Diary | Annequin | 31/08/1918 | 06/09/1918 |
| War Diary | Hohenzollern (North) Sector | 07/09/1918 | 31/10/1918 |
| War Diary | Rumes | 01/11/1918 | 02/11/1918 |
| War Diary | Les Rues Nr. Templeuve. | 03/11/1918 | 14/11/1918 |
| War Diary | Bachy | 15/11/1918 | 30/11/1918 |
| War Diary | Pont-A-Marcq. | 01/12/1918 | 31/05/1919 |

West/1971(3)

West/1571(3)

16TH DIVISION
47TH INFY BDE

18TH BN WELSH REGT.
JLY 1918-MAY 1919

from 119 Bde
40 Div

# WAR DIARY
## or
## INTELLIGENCE SUMMARY

*(Erase heading not required.)*

Army Form C. 2118.

| Hour, Date, Place | Summary of Events and Information | Remarks and references to Appendices |
|---|---|---|
| **1918.** | | |
| ALDERSHOT. July 27. | The First Line Transport consisting of two Officers :- Lt. D.O.Thomas., 2nd.Lt. N.G.Cockaday, and 50 Other Ranks left Bourley Camp for France at 6.0am. | |
| " 29. | The remainder of the Battalion left Government Sidings in two parties at 11.29 pm. and 11.59 pm. for Folkestone. Billetted at Folkestone for the night and embarked for France the following day arriving at Boulogne about 2.0 pm. | |
| BOULOGNE July 30. | Marched up to OSTRHOVE CAMP and stayed the night. | |
| July 31. | Proceeded by Rail to DESVRES and marched to BEZINGHEM area where the Battalion was Billetted. Billets good but scattered. | |
| BEZINGHEM Aug. 1. | Settling in to Billets. | |
| Aug. 2. | Company training all day. | |
| " 3. | Company Training till 12.30 pm. Platoon Cross Country Run in afternoon. Signallers won easily. | |
| " 4. | Church Parade in morning. Fitting Equipment in afternoon. | |
| " 5. | Battalion Training. Showery. | |
| " 6. | Two Companies firing on Range. Two Companies Bathing. Lieut. R.L.Thomas proceeded to 47th. Trench Mortar Battery. Capt. W.T.Davies reported for Duty. | |
| " 7. | Two Companies Firing on Range. Two Companies Bathing. Commenced training bombers in throwing - Lt.G.T.Morris in command. Battalion and Battle Drill - Company training Elementary Outposts. | |
| " 8. | "A" and "B" Companies on Range. | |
| " 9. | "C" and "D" Companies general training. Scouts commenced under Capt. Davies. | |
| " 10. | Inspection of all Companies. Order of Merit (1) C. (2) B. (3) D. (4) A. At about 11.45 am. received orders to be ready to move. Battalion | |

1.

Army Form C. 2118.

# WAR DIARY
## or
## INTELLIGENCE SUMMARY

*(Erase heading not required.)*

Instructions regarding War Diaries and Intelligence Summaries are contained in F.S. Regs., Part II. and the Staff Manual respectively. Title pages will be prepared in manuscript.

| Hour, Date, Place | Summary of Events and Information | Remarks and references to Appendices |
|---|---|---|
| BEZINGHEM. August. 10. cont. | paraded at Headquarters. Notified at about 2.45 pm. that Battalion was under three hours notice to move. Played the 14th Leicesters at football at Doudeauville. Lost 3-nil. Two Companies stayed at Bezinghem and two at Le Fay during the night. | |
| August. 11. | Notice to move cancelled. Companies changed billets i.e. two farthest away being brought nearer to Battalion Headquarters and vice versa, after Divine Services. | |
| " 12. | Two Companies on 100 yards. Range, and two Companies on Battalion Ground Company training. | |
| " 13. | Two Companies on large Range. Two Companies route march and Field operation. Padre Hill left to join Guards, and Padre S.W.A.Collins arrived. | |
| " 14. | Companies training and two Companies on night outposts. Played football against 9th. Black Watch on Battalion Parade Ground. Draw. no score. | |
| " 15. | Two Companies on 100 yards Range. Remainder Company drill. Afternoon recreational training. | |
| " 16. | Commanding Officer attended Inspector General's Conference near HOUCHAIN and witnessed demonstrations in Platoon training. G.O.C. Brigade lectured Seconds in Command, Adjutants and Company Commanders on same subject at PARENTY. Warning order received re going into the Line. 2nd.Lieut. Newton reported. | |
| " 17. | Company Training. Demonstration in Platoon training by Commanding Officer to all Officers. | |
| " 18. | Commanding Officer and Company Commanders proceeded in advance to reconnoitre the Line. Transport moved by road in advance. | |

2.

Army Form C. 2118.

# WAR DIARY
## or
## INTELLIGENCE SUMMARY

*(Erase heading not required.)*

Instructions regarding War Diaries and Intelligence Summaries are contained in F.S. Regs., Part II. and the Staff Manual respectively. Title pages will be prepared in manuscript.

| Hour, Date, Place | Summary of Events and Information | Remarks and references to Appendices |
|---|---|---|
| BEZINGHEM. August. 19. | Battalion embussed at about 7.45 am. and arrived near BARLIN about 4.0 pm. Bivouaced in a cornfield for the night. | |
| " " 20. | Remained in Bivouacs. Commanding Officer inspected Companies. Company Officers and Signal Officer reconnoitred the Line. | |
| " " 21. | Battalion moved by Platoons (first at 9.30am) to line and relieved (1st.Division) 2nd. Welsh in Left Battalion Right Brigade – HOHENZOLLERN SECTOR. "A" and "B" Companies in Front Line. "C" and "D" Companies in support. Relief completed 4.30 pm. "AP SHENKIN." No continuous front line, by series of posts. Transport at Fosse 7 behind BARLIN. Quartermaster's Stores near by. Details left at Divisional Reception Camp at BARLIN. | |
| " " 22. | In the Line. Situation Normal. Casualties – NIL. | |
| " " 23. | Situation normal. Casualties NIL. | |
| " " 24. | 55th Division on left attacked at GIVENCHY after a bombardment, at 7.30 am. Prisoners 65. Slight retaliation on our front causing our first casualty 79397 Pte. R. Sayles "A" Coy. – wounded at Duty. Patrol of one Officer and 6 Other Ranks from "D" Company engaged larger enemy patrol resulting in 2nd.Lt.E.Holmes and 1 Other Rank being wounded and 77508 Pte Jones T. missing. Inter-Company relief. 2nd.Lieut. E. Wolsey wounded whilst proceeding towards the line. | |
| " " 25. | Situation normal. Casualties – NIL. 2nd.Lieut.S.H.Thomas wounded. | |
| " " 26. | Situation normal. Casualties – NIL. | |
| " " 27. | Relieved by 9th Black Watch and took over ANNEQUIN Locality as Battalion in Support. Headquarters in the FOSSE Yard. Left "A" Company in close support to 9th. Black Watch. | |

3.

Army Form C. 2118.

# WAR DIARY
## or
## INTELLIGENCE SUMMARY

*(Erase heading not required.)*

Instructions regarding War Diaries and Intelligence Summaries are contained in F. S. Regs., Part II. and the Staff Manual respectively. Title pages will be prepared in manuscript.

| Hour, Date, Place | Summary of Events and Information | Remarks and references to Appendices |
|---|---|---|
| August 28. | Companies cleaning up and settling down in new quarters. | |
| " 29. | Platoon Training. Very wet during afternoon. | |
| " 30. | Platoon Training, wiring. Also improving posts under R.E. supervision. Weather improved. | |
| ANNEQUIN. " 31. | Platoon Training &c.&c. Improvement of Headquarters accomodation Electric Light &c. "D" Company relieved "A" Company in close support. | |

Wyvern Lieut. Col.,
Commanding 18th. Bn. The Welsh Regt.

# WAR DIARY or INTELLIGENCE SUMMARY

**Army Form C. 2118.**

18th WELSH REGT

| Hour, Date, Place | Summary of Events and Information | Remarks and references to Appendices |
|---|---|---|
| ANNEQUIN September 1st. | Platoon training &c. 2 Prisoners captured by 9th Black Watch taking away sent enemy reconnaissance his front two lines. Received orders as to procedure in case we followed enemy up. | |
| " 2nd. | Prepared to move forward at short notice. Ordinary training carried on with. | |
| " 3. | Inspection of Companies by C.O. Ordinary Platoon training and improvements &c. | |
| " 4. | Ordinary Platoon training and improvements &c. | |
| " 5. | Received Orders to relieve 9th Black Watch in left front (wanal) tomorrow. Preparing for the line, and also ready to move up to support the Black Watch at short notice. | |
| " 6. | Black Watch established post in enemy front line at dawn. We sent up two Companies in early morning & soon after two Companies came up in afternoon seeing like relief the Black Watch had to withdraw from their post. B Co. & A Co. Bat'n remained in the line. We took it as arranged and two men were gassed and went to hospital. | |
| HOHENZOLLERN (NORTH) SECTOR 7. | We took up the new posts on the left, but did not go out to form on the Saunders on our right that had gone forward. | |
| 8. | The Black Watch went back into Reserve, and we took up the Saunders H.Q. 1st man in the Battalion (Pte Freeman) killed by a shell. Situation fairly quiet. 2nd Lieut Rees & Coy while working along a front 6 trench dropped and a enemy bayonet pierced his chin. Had to go to hospital. | |

Army Form C. 2118.

# WAR DIARY
## or
## INTELLIGENCE SUMMARY

(Erase heading not required.)

Instructions regarding War Diaries and Intelligence Summaries are contained in F. S. Regs., Part II. and the Staff Manual respectively. Title pages will be prepared in manuscript.

| Hour, Date, Place | Summary of Events and Information | Remarks and references to Appendices |
|---|---|---|
| September 9th. | "D" Coy relieved "B" Coy on left Company front. Situation quiet. Casualties - Nil. | |
| " 10. | Situation unchanged. Casualties - Nil. | |
| " 11. | 5.30 a.m. the left front Company (D Coy) pushed forward and occupied 3 posts 150', 150' and 300' respectively in advance of our line. They were shelled about 6.30 a.m. "D" Coy H.Qrs. moved up to MUNSTER TUNNEL. Night of 11/12 "D" Coy again advanced its positions in enemy's old trench line in FOSSE TRENCH, also along the RAILWAY. Casualties Lt. R.W. Thompson, gassed. 2lt. P.Coghlan, wounded. No. 6920 Pte. G.Y. Davies - D Coy killed. | |
| " 12. | 1 Boche gave himself up to 8691/8 L/c RADCLIFFE - D Coy. Still holding forward posts which were slightly shelled in early morning. 2nd Lt. W.P. Brown had a slight accident to his knee and went down to C.C.S. The Battalion was relieved at night, and went back to Brigade support. Casualties - Nil. | |
| " 13. | Battalion H.Qrs. moved up to RAILWAY KEEP. Brigade H.Qrs. took up their position in old Battalion H.Qrs. on the RAILWAY EMBANKMENT. Men cleaning up and resting. The Black Watch advanced 400 yds to their own in front of CORONS DE PEKIN. Casualties - 1 O.R. wounded. | |

# WAR DIARY
## INTELLIGENCE SUMMARY

*(Erase heading not required.)*

Army Form C. 2118.

| Hour, Date, Place | Summary of Events and Information | Remarks and references to Appendices |
|---|---|---|
| September 14th. | Men resting and settling down to new quarters. Everything quiet. <br><br> A Coy in GLOSTER KEEP <br> "B" ... RICHMOND POST. <br> "C" ... HENLEY POST. <br> "D" ... SUSSEX POST. <br><br> Casualties - 1 OR. wounded. | |
| 15. | Men resting - nothing special. 3 bursts of 77mm Gas Shell on Bn. H.Qrs. between 10 a.m. and 1 a.m. Enemy stuck to yellow X. <br> Casualties. - No 16203 4/Cpl. MORGAN I. - Died of wounds. <br> No. 46929 Pte. FIELDING R. - GASSED. | |
| 16. | Relieved Black Watch in front line. (Left Front), "A" Coy took over Parados front trench, "B" Coy in Light Support. "C" Coy in Left Support, "D" Coy Reserve at RICHMOND POST. 11.0 p.m. to 2.0 a.m. Enemy shelled RICHMOND POST. <br> Front line both trench shelled at dawn CASUALTIES. - NIL. | |
| 17. | All our posts in position, and consolidated. The Black Watch had suffered heavily and trenches and emplacements were in a much damaged state. Front fairly quiet, with the exception of shells on one of "C" Coy posts. <br> One of our men caught in a Enemy trap - he had to get a piece of iron out of the ground, forthwith and caused an explosion receiving several wounds in leg. <br> Casualties, No. 48298 Pte. HUTCHINSON W. wounded. | |

# WAR DIARY or INTELLIGENCE SUMMARY

Army Form C. 2118.

| Hour, Date, Place | Summary of Events and Information | Remarks and references to Appendices |
|---|---|---|
| September 18. | Situation normal. Companies putting posts in a state of defence. Spade and light railways being pushed forward to front companies. 9/15th m. enemy shelled our front posts and retaliation was called for. At night "D" Coy relieved "A" Coy in front line. "A" Coy going into Reserve. Casualties - 1 OR wounded. | HQ |
| 19. | Quiet day on front. Desultory shelling, we got retaliation. Casualties - 2 OR wounded. | HQ |
| 20. | Situation normal. Rather heavy shrapnel at 9.0 a.m. between Troisor Copse & Orchard. One S.A. came down to about 200 ft. and was out, and was at same time as bombardment - evidently for photography. At night the 9th Black Watch relieved both the Welch and 1st Leicesters taking over Battalion front. Black Watch Battalion HQ at Railway Keep. "A" Coy relieved "B" & "C" Coys, posts as follows:- B Coys in Rt support post. " Lft " Rt " C Coys Front post. " " Lft Support "B" Coy moved back to RICHMOND POST. MUNSTER " DUNDEE " NORTHAMPTON " BERWICK POST. "C" Coy. went into OUNDLE " HENLEY " H.Q. at SIMS KEEP. | HQ |

**Army Form C. 2118.**

# WAR DIARY
## or
## INTELLIGENCE SUMMARY.
(Erase heading not required.)

Instructions regarding War Diaries and Intelligence Summaries are contained in F. S. Regs, Part II. and the Staff Manual respectively. Title pages will be prepared in manuscript.

| Place | Date | Hour | Summary of Events and Information | Remarks and references to Appendices |
|---|---|---|---|---|
| | Sept. 30 cont'd | | "D" Coy moved into SUSSEX POST. HUMANITY. WILSONS GLOSTER. Battalion H.Q. at RAILWAY. Casualties – 30 Killed (2 officers). 20 wounded. | |
| | Oct. 1st | | New posting and relieving up. "A" & "B" & "D" Coys had fairly quiet day. "C" Coy's 6th Brigade took over a trench from 47th Brigade. A Jordan Regiment relieving and held by C. Black Watch. "C" Coy had to close in as follows:– A Coy to RAILWAY KEEP vacated by Black Watch. B " " RICHMOND POST Coy H.Qrs DUNDEE NORTHAMPTON C " GLOSTER D " SUSSEX HUMANITY CROYDEN. Batn. H.Q. did not move. Casualties – NIL. | |

Army Form C. 2118.

# WAR DIARY
## or
## INTELLIGENCE SUMMARY.
(Erase heading not required.)

Instructions regarding War Diaries and Intelligence
Summaries are contained in F. S. Regs., Part II.
and the Staff Manual respectively. Title pages
will be prepared in manuscript.

| Place | Date | Hour | Summary of Events and Information | Remarks and references to Appendices |
|---|---|---|---|---|
|  | Sept. 22 |  | Men cleaning up prior to going out of trenches. A Coy barked Coy Commanders meeting in the morning. At 6.30 p.m. Companies marched off 6 SAILLY LABOURSE & were taken to MARLES-LES-MINES. On arrival guides met A. Coys and showed them their billets. Casualties - 1 O.R. wounded. | R |
|  | 23 |  | Lethury (Natives billets). Distribution of letters in morning. Inspection of Coys by Commanding Officer. Afternoon - Football and Games. | R |
|  | 24 |  | A and B Coys firing on the Range. C. D. Platoon training. Afternoon - Games. | R |
|  | 25 |  | Officers training on Battalion Parade Ground. Afternoon - Recreation training. | R |
|  | 26 |  | Platoon training. Particular attention being given to Patrols. Battle practice. Recreational training. | R |
|  | 27 |  | Moved to Training Ground. Gas Demonstration. Also drawn football. | R |
|  | 28 |  | Kit Inspection and Bath for all Coys. Long route march on usual accuracy. | R |

Army Form C. 2118.

# WAR DIARY
## or
## INTELLIGENCE SUMMARY.
(Erase heading not required.)

Instructions regarding War Diaries and Intelligence Summaries are contained in F. S. Regs., Part II. and the Staff Manual respectively. Title pages will be prepared in manuscript.

| Place | Date | Hour | Summary of Events and Information | Remarks and references to Appendices |
|---|---|---|---|---|
| | Sep. 29. | | Inspection of Boots by Commanding Officer. Divine Service. Lecture on Gas by Lieut Col. MacClean, D.S.O. Tank Corps in HESDIGNEUL. Divisional Concert Party came down to MARLES-LES-MINES and gave a show in the Theatre. | |
| | | 14.30 | Coy. B. Coys on the Range. Ammunition taken up on Great Coats. Platoon Drawing and Company in attack 2nd Battalion. Harry Cinema. Enemy:— Inter Platoon football. Lecture by Senior Linen Officer to Battalion. | |

R. Rumford Inclitor Major
Commanding 8th Welsh Reg't.

# WAR DIARY or INTELLIGENCE SUMMARY

**18th Welsh Regt.** Vol 29

Army Form C. 2118.

| Hour, Date, Place | Summary of Events and Information | Remarks and references to Appendices |
|---|---|---|
| 1st October | 2 & 3 Coys on Range. Fires Contest taken up. Arrival P & B Platoon Training - Boys in attack on Battalion Training Scheme. | |
| 2nd | A & B Coys on Range. 3.5 fired and snapshooting practice. C & D on musketry and medical inspection. The Battalion was listened to by Companies by the Divisional Officer. Football match on Fosse Ground 14 Leicesters v. 18 Welch 2-1. Warning order received to be ready to move off at 4 p.m. notice. | |
| 3 | Troops standing by. Inter Coy and Platoon Football. Order to move received. | |
| 4 | Battalion marched to DROUVIN and billeted in DROUVIN Camp huts. Platoon training in morning. For C & D Coys while A & B were having Baths at HOUCHIN, and while last S.D. were relieved. Afternoon - Programme received C. & D. Coys Bathing | |
| 5 | A & B doing Recreational Training. Rifle & Lewis Gun played 9th Black Watch in afternoon and lost 3.0. | |
| 6 | Inspection of Coys. by Commanding officer. Lecture on range given by P.C.O. in School Room. The Divisional General attended. | |

Army Form C. 2118.

# WAR DIARY
## or
## INTELLIGENCE SUMMARY

*(Erase heading not required.)*

Instructions regarding War Diaries and Intelligence Summaries are contained in F. S. Regs., Part II. and the Staff Manual respectively. Title pages will be prepared in manuscript.

| Hour, Date, Place | Summary of Events and Information | Remarks and references to Appendices |
|---|---|---|
| 7th October | A & B Coys. had a gas stunt under Brigade Gas Officer on training ground – bombs gas being let off afterwards. The new training. C.D. Coys on Range, and also came gas stunt when not actually firing. Warning order received to move. | |
| 8 | Battalion move into billets in CAMBRIN, marching via BEUVRY thence ANNEQUIN. Billet accommodation very limited, and men consequently somewhat cramped. Warning order received to relieve 5th Loyal North Lancs. Battn. moved off at 10.00, and took route via AUCHY 6 CITE de DOUVRIN. Relieved 5th Loyal North Lancs as support Battalion B H.Q. CITE de DOUVRIN. Coys dispositions – Left front. "D" Coy / Right / Left support / Right. | |
| 9 | 1/7 R.H. Ree. relieved 6 & 8 R.H. Rees. 1/4 A Lincolns taken over front line. 10th Welch in support and 9th Black Watch in reserve at ROBERTSONS TUNNEL. Reinforcement of ANNEQUIN. Casualties Nil. | |
| 10 | Men cried shelling and improving position – enemy shelling eased. Quiet day afternoon. Shelling with H.E. and gas round D and B Coys quarters NOT answered. C.O. returned from leave and took over Acting Brigadier. |  |

# WAR DIARY or INTELLIGENCE SUMMARY

(Erase heading not required.)

Army Form C. 2118.

| Hour, Date, Place | Summary of Events and Information | Remarks and references to Appendices |
|---|---|---|
| October 11. | Very quiet day, slight shelling near DOUVRIN, Bryn to Coal & Railway Junction. C.O. & each Company Commander meeting in the evening. Casualties - Nil. | |
| " 12. | Quiet day. Coy Commanders sent up to Grand Fiere to reconnoitre their Company area prior to taking over from 14th Londons. Casualties - 2/Lieut C Smith killed in action at his Platoon post. | ✓ |
| " 13. | Coy Commanders meeting in the morning. Evening we relieved 14 Londons in front line. Bn. H.Q. at STREAM MILL, BILLY. <br> A. Coy. in support at BILLY. <br> B " Right Front Coy in vicinity of DYNAMITE FACTORY. <br> D " Left Front Coy at PREVOTE FARM. <br> C " Centre Coy. at CANAL TEE. <br> At night we sent out a patrol to see if the ground W. of the Canal was occupied. On receiving report all clear we pushed forward two r/cos of C. Coy, one from our section to house at B.13.c. 50.70. and 2 of a section to house at B.13.c. 40.80. B. Coy tried to occupy canal at DYNAMITE FACTORY. but after 3 attempts was driven back by M.G. fire. Casualties - 2nd Lieut S.C. Cook killed by M.G. fire 1 O.R. killed. | 3/ |

# WAR DIARY or INTELLIGENCE SUMMARY

Army Form C. 2118.

*(Erase heading not required.)*

| Hour, Date, Place | Summary of Events and Information | Remarks and references to Appendices |
|---|---|---|
| October 14th. | Quiet day. At nightfall enemy M.G. extremely active. B Coy again attempted to cross Canal but had same result. C Coy. sent out a detail action the DRAWBRIDGE and was fired on from very close range by M.G. 1 O.R. Wounded. | |
| 15. | Orders received B Coy. A and C afterwards (enemy shelled E Bank) was occupied by enemy over fates which reported all clear. C Coy formed bridgehead around DRAWBRIDGE and B Coy. a bridgehead at DYNAMITE FACTORY. After these were established D Coy passed through C and A Coy through B and took up 2nd Bridgehead on Au. C.26 Central — C.20 Central, C.14 Central, then a defence flank facing Canal. A Lewis gun piece was brought now to MG fire in front of PROUVIN. At night defences were G. Century B and A Coys. at Le FAUBOURG of BEUVRY A Coy in Support in Bridgehead B.H.S. moved up to BEUVIN. Casualties 2 O.R. Wounded. | |
| 16. | 9th Black Watch passed through us to take up a pt. position on line D 19 Central — D 19 Central — D 13 Central. 18 LWCh. moved up in support position on line C 16 Central — C 20 Central. Battalion billeted B.H.Q. at FOSSE 1 — C.15a. | |

# WAR DIARY
## or
## INTELLIGENCE SUMMARY
(Erase heading not required.)

Army Form C. 2118.

(5)

| Hour, Date, Place | Summary of Events and Information | Remarks and references to Appendices |
|---|---|---|
| October 16. Contd | In the afternoon orders were received to move forward and attack line to D.7a., D.13 central D.9 central D.25 central with 2 Coys in reserve at D.7.0 a.(c). and B. Coy at D.2.d.6. D.30.A as the 9th Black Watch had pushed forward to the 3rd Objective and met M.G. opposition on line D.8 central D.14 central D.20 coo D.26a oooo. The two front line companies, D Coy left front A. Coy right front. Casualties — Nil. | |
| " 17. | 9th Black Watch reached 3rd Objective and pushed on to the objective along railway in D.26, D.17 and D.18a. Then South in front of PHALEMPIN. Later in the day they advanced the left of their line so as to include the village of WATTIESART. We moved up to above map [along line D.10.6+9, D.23, 6, a., D.28 e.a. with 2 Coys in reserve on line A.10 ic, A.22 a+c D.23 a.o.c. Disposition of Coys. Left front: D. Coy Right: B. Left support: C. Right: A. B. H. O. moved into Chateau in CARNIN. At night the 14 [Irish Regt?] went through the 9th Black Watch & 5th Objective on line E.7 central, E.8 central, E.9 central, E.11.b., E.15.d, E.21.a+c to Dinvinde Railway. Later on night of 17th October orders were received that the 16th Division would move on 18th October. | A 23 ? |

# WAR DIARY or INTELLIGENCE SUMMARY

Army Form C. 2118.

| Place | Date | Hour | Summary of Events and Information | Remarks and references to Appendices |
|---|---|---|---|---|
| | October 18 | | The Divisional Front was divided into two advance guards. The left front being allotted to the 18th Welsh and the Right to Leicesters. The left Advance Guard under Command of Major N. Kyrener V.C. was composed as follows:— 1 Battery 18 Pounders, 1 Sec A.A. Bn M.G.C., 1 Sec 3rd Australian Tunn Coy R.E., 1 Platoon Corps Cyclists, 18 Bn Welsh Regt, Casualties — Nil. It started from its left Advance Guard ay E.1.e.30.60. which but is be found by head of column at 0715 however, owing to a thick ground mist it was somewhat late. The order of march was:— 1 Platoon of "B" Coy forming a screen of scouts, the remaining 3 Platoons together with the ammunition and R.E. moving in extended formation. 1 Section A Coy M.G. columns of platoons C A B H.Q. 1 Battery 18 Pounders 18th Welsh 1st line transport The 65th Div on left & the 15 Div on Right at Divisional Boundary. | |

# WAR DIARY
## INTELLIGENCE SUMMARY.

Army Form C. 2118.

| Place | Date | Hour | Summary of Events and Information | Remarks and references to Appendices |
|---|---|---|---|---|
| | October 19 | | Road taken by AVESNIN – ANTREIUL to ENNEVLIN, at ENNEVLIN opposition encountered from enemy M.G. and Artillery. The line taken up was F3d.a F4c. F5a F6a F11c. formed by B. Coy with C, H & Q. at HELAN. At night B. Coy was relieved by C & D. Coys. A Coy in outpost and B in reserve at ENNEVLIN. B. N. G. established in ENNEVLIN. Casualties 1 O.R. wounded. | |
| | October 19 | | The advance continued through WAHEMY, through COBRIEUX to objective A5 a 99. A 11 6 70 9a. without opposition. A Coy holding the outpost line. B, C & D. in support at COBRIEUX. Later the Brigade moved through the outpost line, B Coy became Battalion in support and with drew A Coy to billets in the village. Casualties — NIL. | |
| | October 20. | | Orders received in the early morning to push forward to final objective T.18 d. 9000 along railway to T 24 c. 0000 than South to T 30 c. 0000. The route taken was near BACHY – SENTIER to RUMES. B Coy's attack extending company light approaching met E. of RUMES from enemy M.G. in the fire but did not prevent the approach being pushed. The civilians in RUMES stated a hostile Cavalry Patrol was in the village to but before retired. The disposition of the Coys – Left Front C Coy. Right Front A Coy. in support D Coy. Left Outpost B Coy. | |

Army Form C. 2118.

# WAR DIARY
## or
## INTELLIGENCE SUMMARY.
(Erase heading not required.)

Instructions regarding War Diaries and Intelligence Summaries are contained in F. S. Regs., Part II. and the Staff Manual respectively. Title pages will be prepared in manuscript.

| Place | Date | Hour | Summary of Events and Information | Remarks and references to Appendices |
|---|---|---|---|---|
| October | 20 cont'd | | Battn. had been consolidated when orders arrived for a further advance to be done in 2 stages. Intermediate front troop line had pushed forward to advance, and so we were almost on the line of R. Bonna. Second bound was (R' Yencourt) TAINTIGNIES (inclusive) UTS central C on R troop being 2 front troop made the advance D & B in support. This advance was without opposition & consolidation B.H.Q. army to railway in the Chateau TAINTIGNIES U 25.8. 0010. A few N.V. shells on village. retrial but on B.H.Q. no damage. Casualties - 1 O.R. wounded M.G. fire. | |
| | 21 | | Left, B.F. Bde Group continued the advance the operation being V.R.C. 0900 MONT de le JUSTICE (inclusive) U.R.L. 09. "A" & "D" Coys. Both wated and other Blin in the day the 14 Sirens also passed through our line moving in rear in reserve. The rain heavy and tearing etc. A Coy lost a foot man open to M.O. noble shelling on TAINTIGNIES and N.W. W night. Casualties 7 O.R. wounded. | |
| | 22 | | TAINTIGNIES - Horizon unchanged still holding position. Sniper shewing on roads in village and Chateau where Brigade H.Qrs. Casualties - Nil. | |
| | 23 | | Company Commanders went up to reconnoitre the line under review to relieve 14 Sercealin in front line position at night. Information of Coy: Right Front Coy - A Coy Left " " - B " Right Support - C " Left " " - D " B.H.Q. Formed at U. 21. A. 6. 30. Casualties - Nil. | |

Army Form C. 2118.

# WAR DIARY
## or
## INTELLIGENCE SUMMARY.
(Erase heading not required.)

| Place | Date | Hour | Summary of Events and Information | Remarks and references to Appendices |
|---|---|---|---|---|
| October | 24 | | A good deal of M.G. fire and irregular shelling along whole front. Batt[alio]n relief had been out on night 23/24 reported being held up by M.G. fire for 2½ hours. She Bocke sent out a Patrol to try and scupper 1 of our posts, but was driven off. Officers of Somerset Light Infantry came up to reconnoitre previous to taking over the line at night. The Battalion was relieved by 6th Somerset Light Infantry in front line position on night 24/25. There was a good deal of shelling on our advanced post and of our area and during the relief. The back areas nearly all had a lot of shelling and the enemy was pretty well strafed somewhere all the way. Casualties 7 O.R. wounded. | |
| | 25 | | The Battalion billeted in RUYES resting and cleaning up. Foot inspection by M.O. Casualties - Nil. | |
| | 26 | | Men getting down to new billets Company Inspection. Officers returned from Brigade and took over Command of the Batt[alio]n. Casualties - Nil. | |
| | 27 | | Divine Service held in Field opposite RUYES Church. Casualties - Nil. | |
| | 28 | | A Coy detailed on Working Party for R.E. on roads. Remainder of Battalion Company Inspection of Clothing, Boots and equipment in morning. In afternoon inspection by C.O. of Coys less 4 Coy | |

# WAR DIARY
## or
## INTELLIGENCE SUMMARY.
*(Erase heading not required.)*

Army Form C. 2118.

| Place | Date | Hour | Summary of Events and Information | Remarks and references to Appendices |
|---|---|---|---|---|
| October | 29 | | Platoon training in Assault Practice Training Ground 7.9 - 8.29.10. (Ref: Sheet 37). C.O. Conference of Company Commanders at 8.30. Casualties - Nil. | |
| | 30 | | C' Coy. was working party on roads under R.E. Remainder of Coys. Platoon training on parade ground. Casualties - Nil. | |
| | 31 | | Bn. on roads as Working Party. A. C. & D. Coys. Platoon training, principally practising advanced guards and patrols. Afternoon - footbal & games. C. O. Conference with Company Commanders. At night a large working party and a K.O. of each with engineers. Casualties - Nil. | |

Wholin Lieut Col
Commanding 15th Welsh Regt

Army Form C. 2118.

# WAR DIARY
## or
## INTELLIGENCE SUMMARY

18th WELSH REGT.

(Erase heading not required.)

Instructions regarding War Diaries and Intelligence Summaries are contained in F. S. Regs., Part II. and the Staff Manual respectively. Title pages will be prepared in manuscript.

| Hour, Date, Place 1918. | Summary of Events and Information | Remarks and references to Appendices |
|---|---|---|
| November 1st. R U M E S. | Platoon Training in the Morning. Football and Games in the afternoon. Casualties – NIL. | |
| November 2. | A, B, & C, Coys. employed digging new line of Trenches, being line of resistance. "D" Company inspected by C.O. & afterwards carried on with Platoon Training. Casualties – NIL. Orders received to move back to billets at LES RUES near Templeuve. | |
| November 3. LES RUES Nr. Templeuve. | The Battalion moved into billets vacated by 22nd Northumberland Fusiliers at LES RUES. The 47th Infantry Brigade being Brigade in Reserve. <br>"A" Company billets at HELEN. <br>"B" Do. Do. ARDOMPREZ. <br>"C" Do. Do. LA QUIEZE. <br>"D" Do. Do. LA QUIEZE. <br>B.H.Q. Do. Do. LES RUES. | |
| November 4. | Battalion settled down to new Billets. Heavy Rain all day. All outdoor training impossible. | |
| " 5. | Very wet day – lectures and indoor training. | |
| " 6. | Platoon training on Company Parade Grounds. Company Drill. Afternoon – Football & Games. | |
| " 7. | Platoon Training suspended owing to heavy rain. Tactical advance scheme – without troops, held by Brigade. Capt. J.P. Jones reported for Duty as reinforcement. | |
| " 8. | Platoon Training by Companies. Afternoon – Recreational Training. | |

Army Form C. 2118.

# WAR DIARY
## or
## INTELLIGENCE SUMMARY

*(Erase heading not required.)*

Instructions regarding War Diaries and Intelligence Summaries are contained in F. S. Regs., Part II. and the Staff Manual respectively. Title pages will be prepared in manuscript.

| Hour, Date, Place | Summary of Events and Information | Remarks and references to Appendices |
|---|---|---|
| November 9. | C.Os. Inspection of Companies in Full Marching Order. A tactical scheme was held for Platoon Commanders. Football and Games in afternoon. Warning order received to move. | |
| " 10. | Battalion ordered to move forward to GUIGNIES. Head of column moved off from LES RUES. 0900. | |
| " 11 | A very trying march owing to amount of traffic on roads – Specially Cavalry. B.H.Q. billeted at Chateau GUIGNES – awfully cold place as no fires were possible. A,B, & C, Companies billeted in Village of GUIGNIES. "D" Coy in WEZ VELVAIN. Commanding Officer left to attend inter Allied Tank Course at Fontainbleu. | |
| " 11. | Parades as usual when news of Armistice having been signed was received. Great jubilation amongst the troops. The G.O.C. Division came round to congratulate everyone. | |
| " 12. | Companies at disposal of Company Commanders – the main thing being recreational Training. The opportunity taken to clean up equipment and billets. The latter were taken over in a very dirty condition. 2Lieut. C. Wyatt reported from Course. | |
| " 13. | As above. Major I.T.Lawrence M.C. returned from Leave. | |
| " 14. | Ceremonial drill and close order Drill. Afternoon devoted to Inter Platoon Football matches. Warning Order received to move. | |
| " 15. BACHY. | Orders to move to BACHY where Battalion billeted for one night. Arrived by 1300 and got nicely settled down before dark. | |

Army Form C. 2118.

# WAR DIARY
## *or*
## INTELLIGENCE SUMMARY

*(Erase heading not required.)*

Instructions regarding War Diaries and Intelligence
Summaries are contained in F.S. Regs., Part II.
and the Staff Manual respectively. Title pages
will be prepared in manuscript.

| Hour, Date, Place | Summary of Events and Information | Remarks and references to Appendices |
|---|---|---|
| November 16. | The Battalion continued to trek starting from Bachy at 0845 and marched via TEMPLEUVE to PONT-A-MARCQ. Frosty and dry. Men came along very well. Arrived at new billeting area in time for dinners. | |
| " 17. | Divine service held in empty tyre Factory. A very cold business as the frost had not given in the slightest. The Brigadier attended the service. The nights following the signing of the Armistice were perfect for Bosche Air Raids, so great pleasure was taken by the troops in exhibiting lights. | |
| " 18. | Platoon Training in morning. Football matches in afternoon had to be cancelled owing to inclement weather. Lieut. Col. W.E.Brown, D.S.O., M.C., rejoined from Inter Allied Tank Course. Reinforcements arrived from Base. | |
| " 19. | 2Lieut.H.S.Davies reported from L.G.School at LE TOUQUET. The Course was washed out after the Armistice. Lectures to Companies on Demobilization Scheme by Battalion Educational Officer. Platoon close order Drill and recreational training. Games. | |
| " 20. | P.T. and Games before Baths. Companies marched to LES RUES in full pack to Divisional Baths. | |
| " 21. | Commanding Officer's inspection of Companies. Games, Recreational Training and a little Ceremonial Drill. | |

# WAR DIARY
## or
## INTELLIGENCE SUMMARY

*(Erase heading not required.)*

Army Form C. 2118.

Instructions regarding War Diaries and Intelligence Summaries are contained in F. S. Regs., Part II. and the Staff Manual respectively. Title pages will be prepared in manuscript.

| Hour, Date, Place | Summary of Events and Information | Remarks and references to Appendices |
|---|---|---|
| November 22. | Recreational Training and close Order Drill. Educational classes in the morning. Afternoon:- Company Soccer League started H.Q. v. "D" Coy. "B" v. "A" Coy. | |
| " 23. | P.T. and Recreational Training. Battalion Drill and Ceremonial. Afternoon Company Soccer League Football. | |
| " 24. | Divine Service held in Brigade Recreation Room. | |
| " 25. | P.T. and Cross Country Running. Close Order & Ceremonial Drill. Afternoon:- Football and Games. | |
| " 26. | Battalion marched to Baths at TEMPLEUVE in full pack. Field Kitchens were taken and dinners served there. | |
| " 27. | Recreational Training. Battalion Drill. Afternoon Games and Football. Lt. G.J.Evans, Lieut. W.G.Greenaway, and 2Lieut. W.G.Jordon for Duty. A Brigade Concert was held at night. A Cross Country run for the Battalion was held in the afternoon. Each Company entering a team of 15 men. "D" Coy had first man home. "C" Coy won team prize. | |
| " 28. | P.T. and Games. Battalion Drill and Ceremonial. Football in the Afternoon. | |
| " 29. | Recreational Training, and Battalion Drill. Football and Games. | |

Army Form C. 2118.

# WAR DIARY
## or
## INTELLIGENCE SUMMARY
*(Erase heading not required.)*

| Hour, Date, Place | Summary of Events and Information | Remarks and references to Appendices |
|---|---|---|
| November 30. | Ceremonial and Physical in morning. Afternoon :- A Brigade Cross Run was held starting from Aerodrome PONT-A-MARCQ. 18th. Welsh and 14th Leicesters were only entries. Leicesters team won. "D" Coy. gave a Company Concert at night. | |

[signature]
Lieut. Col.,
Commanding 18th Bn. Welsh Regt.

Army Form C. 2118.

# WAR DIARY
## or
## INTELLIGENCE SUMMARY.   18th Welsh Regt
*(Erase heading not required.)*

Instructions regarding War Diaries and Intelligence Summaries are contained in F. S. Regs., Part II. and the Staff Manual respectively. Title pages will be prepared in manuscript.

| Place | Date | Hour | Summary of Events and Information | Remarks and references to Appendices |
|---|---|---|---|---|
| PONT-A-MARCQ. | December 1st. | | Divine Service in Brigade Concert Hall. Meeting of Company Sports Officers after. | |
| | December 2nd. | | Recreational Training, Close order drill. Afternoon football, Headquarters v B Company. | |
| | December 3rd. | | Ceremonial Drill, Games. Afternoon, Battalion Match, Welsh v Leicesters latter won 2-1. | |
| | December 4th. | | Morning, Football and Games. Afternoon, Battalion marched to LES RUES for baths, less D Company. | |
| | December 5th. | | D Company went to LES RUES for baths. Remainder of the Battalion, Physical Training, Games and Platoon Training. | |
| | December 6th. | | Ceremonial Drill. Afternoon, Football and Games, mounted paper chase held by Brigade. Starting Point GARGUETELLE. | |
| | December 7th. | | Physical Training and Cross Country Running. Battalion match with 9th. Black Watch, on our ground. We won, 3-2. | |
| | December 8th. | | Sunday. Divine Service in Brigade Concert Hall. | |
| | December 9th. | | Platoon Training and Physical Training. Football match on our ground with A. S. C. they beat us 3-1. D Company moved into Pont-a-Marcq. | |
| | December 10th. | | Battalion marched to Baths at LES RUES. A very wet day. | |

Army Form C. 2118.

# WAR DIARY
## or
## INTELLIGENCE SUMMARY.
*(Erase heading not required.)*

Instructions regarding War Diaries and Intelligence Summaries are contained in F. S. Regs., Part II. and the Staff Manual respectively. Title pages will be prepared in manuscript.

| Place | Date | Hour | Summary of Events and Information | Remarks and references to Appendices |
|---|---|---|---|---|
| PONT-A-MARCQ. | December 11th. | | Orders received to demobilise 79 Coal Miners. Corps Horserace held at MOOCHIN. | |
| | December 12th. | | Very wet. Indoor training. | |
| | December 13th. | | Ceremonial, Physical Training. Afternoon, football and games. | |
| | December 14th. | | Battalion on Salvage work in morning. Afternoon, Divisional Football Competition, 1st. round. Divisional Headquarters v Welsh. We won 6-0. | |
| | December 15th. | | Sunday. Divine Service as usual. | |
| | December 16th. | | Brigade Ceremonial parade ordered but washed out owing to inclement weather. Indoor training instead. | |
| | December 17th. | | Battalion marched to LES RUES for Baths. | |
| | December 18th. | | Physical Training and Company parades. Afternoon, games and football. | |
| | December 19th. | | Physical Training, later ceremonial parade. Football in afternoon. | |
| | December 20th. | | Brigade Ceremonial parade ordered at AVELIN, but washed out owing to rain. Battalion ceremonial parade after it cleared up. Lt. G. E. Markham for duty after sick leave. | |

Army Form C. 2118.

# WAR DIARY
## or
## INTELLIGENCE SUMMARY.
(Erase heading not required.)

Instructions regarding War Diaries and Intelligence Summaries are contained in F. S. Regs., Part II. and the Staff Manual respectively. Title pages will be prepared in manuscript.

| Place | Date | Hour | Summary of Events and Information | Remarks and references to Appendices |
|---|---|---|---|---|
| PONT-A-MARCQ. | | | | |
| | December 21st. | | Battalion on Salvage in the morning 2nd round of Divisional League, 18th Welsh v Tyneside Scottish at Templeuve. Tyneside Scottish won 3-1. | |
| | December 22nd. | | Divine Service in Brigade Concert Hall. A very wet day. | |
| | December 23rd. | | Indoor training owing to rain. | |
| | December 24th. | | Getting Christmas stores from the Canteen, and decorating billets. | |
| | December 25th. | | Church Parade. The C.O. rode round all companies to wish the men the compliments of the season and to see the dinners. | |
| | December 26th. | | No training, recovering from the effects of the previous day. | |
| | December 27th. | | Battalion detailed for Salvage but owing to heavy rain it was cancelled. | |
| | December 28th. | | Kit inspection for all companys. Physical Training. B Company detailed as wiring party for Divisional Salvage Dump. A very wet day. | |
| | December 29th. | | Church Parade in Brigade Concert Hall. | |

Army Form C. 2118.

# WAR DIARY
## or
## INTELLIGENCE SUMMARY.
*(Erase heading not required.)*

| Place | Date | Hour | Summary of Events and Information | Remarks and references to Appendices |
|---|---|---|---|---|
| PONT-A-MARCQ. | December 30th. | | B Company wiring on Divisional Dump, salvage, A, C, & D. Companys at lecture on "Individual and National Health: Afternoon Inter company football. | |
| | December 31st. | | Battalion marched to LES RUES for baths. Football and games in afternoon. | |

Major,
Commanding 18th. Bn. Welsh Regt.

Army Form C. 2118.

# WAR DIARY
or
## INTELLIGENCE SUMMARY.
*(Erase heading not required.)*

18 Welsh

Instructions regarding War Diaries and Intelligence Summaries are contained in F. S. Regs., Part II. and the Staff Manual respectively. Title pages will be prepared in manuscript.

| Place | Date | Hour | Summary of Events and Information | Remarks and references to Appendices |
|---|---|---|---|---|
| PONT-A-MARCQ. | January 1st. 1919. | | New Years Day. Parades as usual, salvage work in morning by whole Battalion. Afternoon, Leicesters v. 18th Welsh on our ground. We lost 3-1. | |
| | January 2nd. | | Physical Training and Company Drill. Education and Games | |
| | January 3rd. | | Physical Training & Education. Battalion Ceremonial Drill on 'C' Company's Football Ground at LE TREUPE. | |
| | January 4th. | | Kit Inspection and Physical Training. Afternoon, Boxing Contests in Tyre Factory at PONT-A-MARCQ. | |
| | January 5th. | | Divine Service in Brigade Concert Hall. 2Lt. Gaughan proceeded on leave. | |
| | January 6th. | | Lectures on Demobilization in Tyre Factory, PONT-A-MARCQ A & C first then B & D. | |
| | January 7th. | | Physical Training and Education. | |
| | January 8th. | | Physical Training and Education. Battalion on Salvage Work. Recreational Training & Games. | |
| | January 9th. | | Physical Training and Education. Company Training, football in afternoon. | |
| | January 10th. | | Physical Training and Education. 'A' & 'C' Coys. on Ceremonial Drill. 'B'& 'D' attended a Lecture on Colonial Development at 14th Leicesters. (TOURMIGNIES) | |
| | January 11th. | | Physical Training and Education. C.Os inspection of Company's. Football & Games. | |
| | | | Physical Training & Education. Kit Inspection by Coys. Afternoon, Div. Signals v 18th Welsh at AVELIN result a draw 1-1. 34 men demobilized also Lt.P.A.Lewis, 2Lt.L.H.WATTS and 2Lt. MC.DONAGH. | |
| | January 12th. | | Divine Service in Brigade Concert Hall. | |
| | JANUARY 13th. | | 'B' Company constructing a miniature range at LA MOOSERIE. 'D' Company on Salvage clearing shells from LA MOOSERIE Dump. | |
| | January 14th. | | Battalion marched to LES RUES for baths. Lt.W.J.McGubbin went on leave. | |
| | January 15th. | | 'B' Company went on Range (firing). Remainder clearing LA MOOSERIE ammunition dump. | |
| | January 16th. | | C.Os inspection of companies. Physical Training & Education. Working on ammunition dumps | |
| | January 17th. | | Physical Training & Education. Battalion on Salvage. | |
| | January 18th. | | Physical Training & Education. 'A' Company moved from LE CROQUET to billets at PONT-A-MARCQ. 24 men demobilized also 2Lt. E.L.DAVIES, and 2LT.J.L. NEWTON. Final of Div.League, 14th Leicesters v. R.I. Fuslrs. | |

Army Form C. 2118.

# WAR DIARY
## or
## INTELLIGENCE SUMMARY.
*(Erase heading not required.)*

Instructions regarding War Diaries and Intelligence Summaries are contained in F.S. Regs. Part II. and the Staff Manual respectively. Title pages will be prepared in manuscript.

| Place | Date | Hour | Summary of Events and Information | Remarks and references to Appendices |
|---|---|---|---|---|
| PONT-A-MARCQ. | January 19th. | | Divine Service in Brigade Concert Hall. 2Lt Cockaday proceeded on leave. | |
| | January 20th. | | Physical Training and Education, Salvage, Football & Games. | |
| | January 21st. | | The Battalion marched to LES RUES for baths. Education, Football & Games. Lt.G.T.Morris proceeded on leave to U.K. | |
| | January 22nd. | | 'A'Coy. Physical Training. 'B'Coy. on Range. 'B'Coy working party for House Sale at PONT-A-MARCQ. 'C'Coy moved to FRETIN to act as 1 Corps Guard on trains, moving forward. Football & Games. Education. | |
| | January 23rd. | | 'A'& 'B'Coys lecture on 'Citizenship' by the Rev. S.W.A.Collins. Physical Training. 'D'Coy moved to FRETIN to reinforce 'C'Coy as 1Corps Guard. 'A'& 'B'Coys, Football & Games, Education. | |
| | January 24th. | | 'A'& 'B'Coys Physical Training and Salvage Work. Football & Games, Education. 'C' & 'D' Coys 1stCorps train Guard at FRETIN. Lt.J.L.Pawdon proceeded to U.K. on leave. | |
| | January 25th. | | 'A'& 'B'Coys Physical Training and Kit Inspection. Football & Games & Education. 'C', 'D' Coys - at FRETIN 1Corps Guard. Lieut. DICKINSON and 76 other ranks were demobilised Lt.&Q.M.&Q.M.G.H.Jones Lt.A.D.Grant, and 2Lt.T.Edwards proceeded to U.K. as draft conducting officers. | |
| | January 26th. | | Divine Service in Brigade Concert Hall. | |
| | January 27th. | | 'A'& 'B'Coys Physical Training and Salvage Work, working party of 1N.C.O. and 30 O.Rs. for Work at Coal Dump unloading lorries. 'C'& part of 'D'Coy 1Corps Guard at FRETIN. Two O.Rs, for Demobilization. Lt.C.E.Markham proceeded to H.Qrs, L of C Area, PARIS for duty. Thirty five O.Rs. returned from 1Corps Guard at FRETIN. | |
| | January 28th. | | 'A'& 'B'& part of 'D'Coys Physical Training and Battalion Ceremonial Drill. Football & Games Education. 'C'Coy and part of 'D' 1st Corps Guard at FRETIN. 13 O.Rs, demobilized. | |
| | January 29th. | | 'A' & 'B'. and part of 'D' Coys Brigade Ceremonial Parade. Football & Games, Education. 'C' & part of 'D' Coys at FRETIN 1Corps Guard. | |
| | January 30th. | | 'A'. & 'B' & part of 'D' Coys Physical Training and Battalion Ceremonial Drill. Football & Games, Education. 'C' & 'B' Coys relieved by 14thLeicesters at FRETIN and moved into billets at PONT-A-MARCQ. | |
| | January 31st. | | Brigade Ceremonial Parade. Divl. Boxing Competition commenced. Football & Games, Education. | |

...................... MAJOR.
Cmdg. 18th. Bn. The Welsh Regt.

18 Welsh Rgt. Army Form C. 2118.
Vol 33

# WAR DIARY
or
## INTELLIGENCE SUMMARY.
(Erase heading not required.)

| Place | Date | Hour | Summary of Events and Information | Remarks and references to Appendices |
|---|---|---|---|---|
| Antwerp | February 1/19/19 | | Brigade Ceremonial. No football owing to heavy snow. | |
| | February 2" | | H.R.H. Prince of Wales visited Antwerp during along of the Brit. Army. H.Q.H. called at the mess of Major Lawrence in Berkhause. O.C. 16 Coy. was presented, also Adjt. H.R.H. reviewed down ranks, stock as for as Bde. H.Q. He stopped several times on the way to speak to men chiefly those with ribbons or stripes. Divine service during morning. | |
| | February 3rd | | The Brigade paraded on Aerodrome, formed in hollow square for presentation of Kings Colours. Bach Battalion by H.R.H. Prince of Wales. The colours were Consecrated beforehand. H.R.H. made an address. Battalion then marched past ceremony concluded with an advance by the Brigade in Review Order. | |
| | February 4" | | Company training, working parties, salvage. also. | |
| | February 5" | | Working parties, Salvage, etc. Capt. Thruston + 2Lt. Williams proceeded on conducting duties with demobilized men. Capt. B. Jones proceeded to Berlin to assume duties as Town Major. | |
| | January 6" | | Working parties, Salvage, fatigues. The weaths too bad for football. | |

Army Form C. 2118.

# WAR DIARY
or
## INTELLIGENCE SUMMARY.
(Erase heading not required.)

Instructions regarding War Diaries and Intelligence Summaries are contained in F. S. Regs., Part II. and the Staff Manual respectively. Title pages will be prepared in manuscript.

| Place | Date | Hour | Summary of Events and Information | Remarks and references to Appendices |
|---|---|---|---|---|
| Contay. | | | | |
| | February 7th/19 | | Battalion formed into two companies today. No 1. Platoon formed of remainder of A. Coy. | |
| | | | 2,3,4th Platoons formed of other H.Qrs. companies. Non O.R.s demobilyzed today. Coy. returned from leave. | |
| | February 8th/19 | | Kit Inspection. Lecture by Capt Young. "Retention in Army for Armies of occupation." | |
| | February 9th " | | Divine Service. | |
| | February 10th " | | Physical Training - Inspection Major Lawrence - proceed on leave. | |
| | February 11th " | | Companies marched to baths at Templeuve | |
| | February 12th " | | P.T. Arms drill, drill lecture. Lectures during afternoon. | |
| | February 13th " | | " " " " " " " " 26 O.R.s demobilized 2 N.C. Officers | |
| | February " | | Arms drill Lecture Drill all during afternoon. | |
| | | | proceeded as Draft Conducting Officer | |
| | February 14th " | | P.T. Arms drill, etc. Lt Greensway + 8 O.Rs demobilyzed. | |
| | February 15th " | | P.T. Arms drill Etc. 3 O.Rs demobilyzed. | |
| | February 16th " | | Divine Services. | |
| | February 17th " | | P.T. Arms drill Etc. L/Bo. Horrocks + Hospital Lt. Morris Surrendered + 58 O.Rs Killi. | |
| | February 18th " | | Band. Duties. | |
| | | | Battalion made use of new Buds which have been constructed in H. Ayr Factory. 7 men demobilized. | |

# WAR DIARY or INTELLIGENCE SUMMARY

Army Form C. 2118.

| Place | Date | Hour | Summary of Events and Information | Remarks and references to Appendices |
|---|---|---|---|---|
| Bois d'Nieppe | February 19th, 1919 | | P.T. Salvage. Two O.Rs demobilized | |
| | February 20th | | P.T. Running Exercise. Salvage. Lt. H. Evans Henglanf. ex draft Commanding Officer | |
| | February 21st | | C.O.'s Inspection, advised that the ground & 2 x 6 Evans had been demobilized whilst on leave. | |
| | February 22nd | | P.T. Lectires. Salvage. 3 men demobilized | |
| | February 23rd | | Divine Service. 2 ORs demobilized | |
| | February 24th | | P.T. Running Exercise. Salvage | |
| | February 25th | | P.T. Running Exercise. Salvage. Afternoon Games. | |
| | February 26th | | P.T. Running Exercise. Salvage. Lecture by Capt. Young on Recruitment | |
| | February 27th | | Bathing. Afternoon Games. 20 ORs demobilized. | |
| | February 28th | | Physical Training. Route march. Working Parties. Afternoon Games. | |

W.M. Evans Lieut. Col.
Comdg. 18th Bn. The Welsh Regt.

Army Form C. 2118.

# WAR DIARY
## INTELLIGENCE SUMMARY.
*(Erase heading not required.)*

Instructions regarding War Diaries and Intelligence Summaries are contained in F. S. Regs., Part II. and the Staff Manual respectively. Title pages will be prepared in manuscript.

18 W(elsh)

HEADQUARTERS
2 APR 9

9/5 34

| Place | Date | Hour | Summary of Events and Information | Remarks and references to Appendices |
|---|---|---|---|---|
| Fort a Cinay | 1/3/19 | | Physical Training. Kit Inspection. | |
| | 2/3/19 | | Divine Service. Afternoon. Same. | |
| | 3/3/19 | | Physical Training. Arms Drill. Working Party of 20 other ranks to Salvage Work. | |
| | 4/3/19 | | Bathing. Brig. Gen. B.C. Dent. Commanding 47th Infantry Brigade proceeded to England to take over command of the 2nd Leicester Bath. Lt Col W.S.Browne D.S.O., M.C. acting as Brigadier. | |
| | 5/3/19 | | Commanding Officer's Inspection. Physical Training. Working Party of 20 other ranks found. | |
| | 6/3/19 | | Educational Lecture. Inspection of Arms Equipment and Clothing. | |
| | 7/3/19 | | Physical Training. Arms drill and Educational Lecture. 10 other ranks demobilized. | |
| | 8/3/19 | | Inspection of draft for the 16" Welsh Reg and cleaning of Clothing equipment etc. | |
| | 9/3/19 | | Draft of 3 Officers and 150 other ranks proceeded to join 16" Welsh Reg. Divine Service. | |
| | 10/3/19 | | Preparing further draft of 2 officers and 50 other ranks to proceed to 16" Welsh Reg. | |
| | 11/3/19 | | Draft of 2 officers and 50 other ranks proceeded to join 16" Welsh Reg. | |
| | 12/3/19 | | Reorganizing battalion and Inspection. | |
| | 13/3/19 | | Bathing and cleaning up dress etc. 2 Battalion and 20 other ranks demobilized. | |

# WAR DIARY
## or
## INTELLIGENCE SUMMARY.
*(Erase heading not required.)*

Army Form C. 2118.

| Place | Date | Hour | Summary of Events and Information | Remarks and references to Appendices |
|---|---|---|---|---|
| Bud-a-huy | 14/3/19 | | Clearing up stores and preparing to move transport to Zenghem. | |
| | 15/3/19 | | Clearing up stores and checking half equipment prior to moving same to Zenghem. | |
| | 16/3/19 | | do do do | |
| | 17/3/19 | | 2/Capt W.J. Davies, 2/Capt J.S. Guilford and 2nd Lt J.J. Edwards and 67th demobilized. | |
| | 18/3/19 | | Clearing up stores and preparing to move transport & half equipment to Zenghem. | |
| | 19/3/19 | | Commenced moving transport and Mob equipment to Zenghem. | |
| | 19/3/19 | | Moving transport and Mob equipment to Zenghem. | |
| | 20/3/19 | | do do do completed. | Baths. |
| | 21/3/19 | | do do do | |
| | 22/3/19 | | Clearing up stores, billets and transport lines. | |
| | 23/3/19 | | do do | |
| | 23/3/19 | | Major Gen. A.B. Ritchie C.B., C.M.G. relinquishes command of the 16th Division. | |
| | 24/3/19 | | Commanding officers Inspection and Pay Parade. | |
| | 25/3/19 | | Clearing and doing transport at Zenghem. 16th Division replaced by 16th Brigade. | |
| | | | Headquarters House. Lt. A. McCullagh, Lieut Rice Collins, Lieut G.J. Hinno | |
| | | | and 6 other ranks demobilized. | |
| | 26/3/19 | | Clearing and doing transport at Zenghem. | |

**Army Form C. 2118.**

# WAR DIARY
## or
## INTELLIGENCE SUMMARY.
(Erase heading not required.)

Instructions regarding War Diaries and Intelligence Summaries are contained in F. S. Regs., Part II. and the Staff Manual respectively. Title pages will be prepared in manuscript.

| Place | Date | Hour | Summary of Events and Information | Remarks and references to Appendices |
|---|---|---|---|---|
| Bodn Lung | 27/3/19 | | First Horse replaced by Donor Cobs under Brig Gen L.G. Howell | |
| | 28/3/19 | | G.D. & W. G. RA. Battn. | |
| | | | Cleaning and oiling transport at Ceroplane. Inspection of clothing and equipment. | |
| | 29/3/19 | | Rifle Inspection and cleaning of billets. | |
| | 30/3/19 | | Church Parade for Divine Service. Col A. Cathars, Lieut A. Gardner, Lieut | |
| | | | I. Chaubrate and 11 other ranks dismelope. | |
| | 31/3/19 | | Inspection of all ranks by the commanding officer. Col G.W. Aubrey discharge from Hospital and returned to duty with Battalion being relinquished the post of Area Commandant at Attiche | |
| | 31/3/19 | | | |

[signature] Lieut Col.
Commanding 1st Battalion
The Welsh Regt.

18 Welch R.  Army Form C. 2118.

WAR DIARY
or
INTELLIGENCE SUMMARY.
(Erase heading not required.)

| Place | Date | Hour | Summary of Events and Information | Remarks and references to Appendices |
|---|---|---|---|---|
| Port a Mouq | 1/4/19 | | Cleaning equipment and inspection of same | |
| | 2/4/19 | | Inspection by Commanding Officer | |
| | 3/4/19 | | Baths. Lt Col W.C. Brown DSO MC proceeded to U.K. on leave | |
| | 4/4/19 | | Cleaning Billets | |
| | 5/4/19 | | Physical Training. For other ranks demobilized | |
| | 6/4/19 | | Church Parade | |
| | 7/4/19 | | Cleaning Limbers at Employment. Pay Parade | |
| | 8/4/19 | | Physical Training and Arms Drill | |
| | 9/4/19 | | Commanding Officers' Inspection | |
| | 10/4/19 | | Baths | |
| | 11/4/19 | | Cleaning Billets | |
| | 12/4/19 | | Kit Inspection | |
| | 13/4/19 | | Church Parade | |
| | 14/4/19 | | Cleaning Limbers at Employment. Pay Parade | |
| | 15/4/19 | | Physical Drill and Arms Drill | |
| | 16/4/19 | | Commanding Officers' Inspection | |

# WAR DIARY
## or
## INTELLIGENCE SUMMARY.
(Erase heading not required.)

Army Form C. 2118.

| Place | Date | Hour | Summary of Events and Information | Remarks and references to Appendices |
|---|---|---|---|---|
| Bout au kanoy | 17/4/19 | | Baths | |
| | 18/4/19 | | 1 Officer and 6 other ranks proceeded by lorry to Brussels and endeavour to return on the 20th inst. Instructions received for all troops to have a holiday until the 22nd inst. | |
| | 19/4/19 | | 6 other ranks proceeded to Lille for the day | |
| | 20/4/19 | | Church Parade. Lt. Col. W.E. Brown DSO, M.C. rejoined from leave. Capt. G.W. Asher on leave to U.K. | |
| | 21/4/19 | | Orders received for 36 other ranks to proceed to the 16" Welsh Rgt. 2nd Lt. S.C. Webb Reid | |
| | 22/4/19 | | 22 other ranks proceeded to 16" Welsh Rgt and 14 otherranks detached were cross posted | |
| | | | Baths | |
| | 23/4/19 | | Lieut. W.J. Evans proceeded on leave | |
| | | | Commanding Officers inspection | |
| | 24/4/19 | | Cleaning billets | |
| | 25/4/19 | | Physical training and Bruno drill. Pay Parade | |
| | 26/4/19 | | Kit Inspection | |
| | 27/4/19 | | Church Parade | |

Army Form C. 2118.

# WAR DIARY
## INTELLIGENCE SUMMARY.
*(Erase heading not required.)*

Instructions regarding War Diaries and Intelligence Summaries are contained in F. S. Regs., Part II. and the Staff Manual respectively. Title pages will be prepared in manuscript.

| Place | Date | Hour | Summary of Events and Information | Remarks and references to Appendices |
|---|---|---|---|---|
| Intra-Iraq | 28/4/19 | | Baku | |
| | 29/4/19 | | Commanding Officers Inspection | |
| | 30/4/19 | | Cleaning titles weather very wet. | |

J. Rumford Jones Capt
Commanding 18 Battalion
Welsh Regt.

Army Form C. 2118.

18 Welsh Pg6

Vol 36

# WAR DIARY
## or
## INTELLIGENCE SUMMARY.
(Erase heading not required.)

Instructions regarding War Diaries and Intelligence Summaries are contained in F. S. Regs., Part II. and the Staff Manual respectively. Title pages will be prepared in manuscript.

| Place | Date | Hour | Summary of Events and Information | Remarks and references to Appendices |
|---|---|---|---|---|
| Pott – a | 1/5/19. | | Physical Training. | |
| Marcq. | 2/5/19. | | Baths and Pay parade. | |
| | 3/5/19. | | Kit Inspection | |
| | 4/5/19. | | Divine Service | |
| | 5/5/19. | | Clothing and Equipment inspection, 3 other ranks demobilized. | |
| | 6/5/19. | | Inspection by the Adjutant. | |
| | 7/5/19. | | Cleaning Billets | |
| | 8/5/19. | | Cleaning Wagons at Templeuve, 3 other ranks demobilized, | |
| | 9/5/19. | | Baths and Pay parade. | |
| | 10/5/19. | | A party of 1 Officer and 9 other ranks proceeded to Brussels for 3 days by Motor Lorry. | |
| | 11/5/19. | | Church Parade. | |
| | 12/5/19 | | Clothing and Equipment inspected. | |
| | 13/5/19. | | Inspection by the Commanding Officer. | |
| | 14/5/19. | | Cleaning Billets. | |
| | 15/5/19. | | Physical Training. | |
| | 16/5/19. | | Baths and Pay parade. | |
| | 17/5/19. | | Kit inspection, Lieut. & Q.M. G.H.Jones proceeded on leave to U.K. Lieut. Col. W.E.Brown D.S.O. M.C. proceeded on leave to Cologne for 7 days. | |
| | 18/5/19. | | Church Parade. | |
| | 19/5/19. | | Inspection by the Commanding Officer. | |
| | 20/5/19. | | Working on Wagons at Templeuve to prevent spokes loosening through the heat. | |
| | 21/5/19. | | do do do do do | |
| | 22/5/19. | | do do do do do | |
| | 23/5/19 | | Pay parade. A/Capt. T.Young proceeded to England for demobilization. | |
| | 24/5/19. | | Kit. inspection. | |
| | 25/5/19. | | Church service in the evening. | |
| | 26/5/19. | | Inspection by the Commanding Officer. | |
| | 27/5/19. | | Cleaning Billets. | |
| | 28/5/19. | | Baths | |
| | 29/5/19. | | 2 horses and limber proceeded to Seclin to remove stores of 230 Coy. R.E. to Templeuve. | |
| | 30/5/19. | | Pay Parade. | |
| | 31/5/19. | | Kit inspection. | |

W Renton Lieut. Col.
Comdg. 18th Bn. The Welsh Regt.

www.ingramcontent.com/pod-product-compliance
Lightning Source LLC
Chambersburg PA
CBHW081456160426
43193CB00013B/2501